Condition Hacking

Blindspot Profits: Profiting Off Overlooked Items Every Seller Misses, and the Hidden Fortune All Around You

First published digitally in February 2015 by Mastery Media.
First paperback edition published 2019 by Mastery Media.

All rights reserved. No part of this book or site may be reproduced or redistributed in any form or by any electronic or mechanical means, including information storage and retrieval systems, without permission in writing from the author and publisher, except by a reviewer who may quote brief passages in a review.

Copyright © 2019 Peter Valley

www.FBAmastery.com

peter@fbamastery.com

Table of Contents

Section I: The role of condition in your Amazon profits

Condition hacking 101: How this book will make you money	5
That book of yours would have sold if you knew how to fix it	6
The mind of the Amazon buyer: Why condition matters	7
About me: The story of how I learned all these cool Jedi tricks	7
When I use these tricks: My criteria	8
Why listing in Acceptable condition is almost the same as it not being for sale at all	9
Making books new again? A: Yes.	9
The special case of textbooks	12
Very Good vs. Good condition: Does it matter?	12
Books that appeal to Collectors versus those that appeal to everyone else	13
The benefits of grading conservatively	15
Your condition hacking toolbox	16
How to use this book	18

Section II: How to restore a book to New condition. If you have a book that is New except for one of these blemishes – here's how to fix them.

I have a book with...

Ink on the cover	20
A dirty or dusty exterior	20
An irremovable blemish on a blank or unnecessary page	20
A price written in the corner of the first page	21
A damaged dust jacket	22
Ink in the corner of a title page (e.g. price marked in pen, owner's name, etc)	22
Writing or ink on one or more pages	23
A cover that has lost its shine	23
A stain or blemish on the back cover	24
A fold to the corner of a page	24
A remainder mark	24

Section III: How to upgrade a book to Good (or Very Good) condition. If you have a book that is Acceptable because of a defect listed here – your solution has arrived.

I have a book with...

A tilted spine.	27
A severely split or feathered corner or corners (most effective with hardcovers)	27
A curved cover of hardcover book	27
A reeeeally bad smell	28

An extremely torn or damaged dust jacket	29
A smudge mark on the cover of a cloth hardcover book.	29
Highlighting	29

Section IV: How to upgrade a book to Very Good condition. If you have a book that is merely Good – here's how to get it up to Very Good.

I have a book with…

A grease stain on a cloth cover.	32
Pages marked with White Out	32
Stickers or sticker residue on the front or back cover.	32
A book plate on the inside cover or one of the first pages.	32
A dust jacket that has wrinkles, folds, or waves	33

Section V: How to turn a damaged, unsellable book into one you can turn into money.

I have a book with…

A cover or back cover that reads "Promotional Copy Only – Not for Sale."	35
A page torn out	35
A batch of pages that have been torn out	35
Water damage	36
Major damage that is literally falling apart, has a cover torn off, or has other massive structural damage	36

Section VI: The science of library book repair: With these tricks, no one will know your book came from a library.

I have a book with…

A library call number written on the spine	40
A ton of library stickers and stamps on a plastic slipcover	40
A library pocket	41
A library book plate on the inside cover or first page	41
A library ink stamp inside	41
A library bar code sticker or other stickers	42
A customer thinks you stole a library book	42

Section VII: Bonus: Other tricks for increasing the value of books & other media

Books: Selling as another, identical edition	44
Books, CDs, & DVDS: Using redundant product pages	44
DVDs: Purchasing incomplete sets	45
Books: Common books that can be batched into sets and sold profitably	45
CDs & DVDs: Torn shrink-wrap	46
CDs & DVDs: Repairing damaged discs	46
CDs & DVDs: Replacing damaged cases	47
CDs & DVDs: Batching items with missing artwork and selling on eBay	47

Section I
The role of condition in your Amazon profits

Condition hacking 101: How this book will make you money
That book of yours would have sold if you knew how to fix it
The mind of the Amazon buyer: Why condition matters
About me: The story of how I learned all these cool Jedi tricks
When I use these tricks: My criteria
Making books new again? A: Yes.
Very Good vs. Good condition: Does it matter?
Why listing in Acceptable condition is almost the same as it not being for sale at all
Books that appeal to Collectors versus those that appeal to everyone else
The benefits of grading conservatively
Your condition hacking toolbox
How to use this book

Condition hacking 101: How this book will make you money

You're an Amazon customer. You're ready to drop $75 on an obscure academic press title published by University of Alaska in 1984. There are four used copies for sale, each priced at $75.

One is listed as "Good condition." The condition notes read: "Ex-library book. Has usual stamps and labels. Light handling wear."

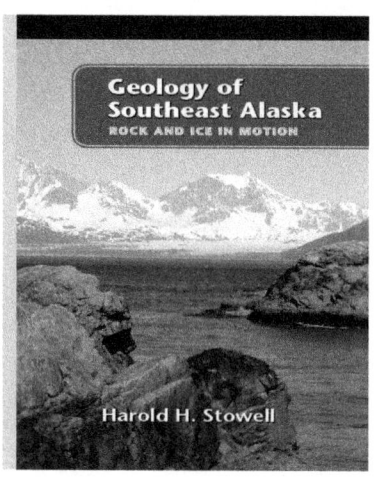

Another is listed as "Very good condition." The condition notes read; "Has pen markings on front cover. Otherwise new condition."

Another is listed as "Acceptable condition." Condition notes read: "Pencil marks on five pages. Dust jacket has many tears and extremely heavy wear."

Another is listed as "Good condition." Condition notes read: "Average used copy. Average handling wear. No writing or highlighting."

Which one do you buy?

Each of the respective sellers has $75 on the line (minus commissions). Each copy is priced the same.

How do you decide?

One variable is seller feedback. The seller with 99% positive feedback might beat out the seller with 92% feedback, even if his copy is in worse condition. But repairing your feedback is not what this book is about. (That's what this other book is about).

Setting that aside. How do you decide?

You might simply go for the offer at the top of the listings. The factors that contribute to this are whether or not the seller uses Fulfillment by Amazon, their feedback score, and the book's condition. All other things being equal, the book with the best condition gets the top spot, and is most likely to get the sale.

But you're spending $75 on a book, and aren't as likely to make a rush decision. You're spending some money, so you'll at least take the time to review your options.

Some would make a rush assessment and assume the copy in the highest condition category would get the sale. In the above instance, that would be the one listed as "Very Good."

But look closer at that listing. "Pen markings on front cover." For one, if the seller was scrupulous, she probably shouldn't have listed this as Very Good. That type of very visible blemish is more safely listed as "Good Condition," even though the book is otherwise a new copy.

That aside, the buyer may be more sensitive about pen marks on the cover of an otherwise new book than more serious damage concealed inside. Maybe she's using the book in a reading group, and she doesn't want to wave around a blemished book with someone's name on it in front of her colleagues. It just looks weird. Or she's using it for a class, and the professor specifically forbade purchasing used copies. She's breaking the rules, but he's none the wiser if there are no obvious and huge exterior blemishes that scream "used copy" from across the room.

Most will rule out the Acceptable copy right off the top. It's the worst condition there is on Amazon, and almost all buyers know it.

The ex-library copy is going to freak out a lot of buyers. Just the fact that a book is a retired library copy is going to significantly affect the likelihood it will sell.

Fact is, the last listing is going to get the sale most of the time. It's "Good Condition," (and not VG or LN), but it's by far the least offensive offer. It is quite simply a lightly used copy, with no real reason for anyone to pass on it.

Now, anyone who understands how important condition is in a buying decision can exaggerate the condition they list their book in. They can take a Very Good book and list as New. They can take an Acceptable copy and list as Good. But sellers who deceive customers won't last. They will be punished in the form of negative feedback, and if they continue, will be driven off Amazon altogether.

But there's one giant caveat

Any one of these offers could have been the winner. The blemishes in every book could have been corrected, and the condition of each could have been increased at least one level above, making it the one that sold.

The person selling the ex-library book could have erased any sign it had ever come from a library, raising it to a Very Good copy.

The person selling the VG copy with Sharpie writing on the dust jacket could have removed any trace of the pen marks, raising it to a New copy.

The Acceptable copy could have had the pencil marks removed, and the dust jacket replaced with a generic but perfect one, making the copy worthy of a Good condition listing.

If they had taken the time, the sale could have gone to any of these sellers.

That's what I'm here to cover.

The mind of the Amazon buyer: Why condition matters

Sellers have far too much confidence in the Buy Box and the top listing, and thinking if they have these, they have the sale. And this is usually the case with high-demand books. Yet we underestimate the savvy of the Amazon buyer, and the extent that they review their options before making a purchase. The internet is a fast-paced, instant-gratification environment, but not so much that they're buying your highlighted, war-torn copy of *Getting to Yes* just because it holds the top spot.

I have monitored many offers in Acceptable condition, and watched non-Acceptable offers lower down the list sell while my Acceptable offer languished. It's noticeable even with decently-ranked books. And the problem gets even more serious the lower the demand for the book. (I cover what a "good" and "bad" Sales Rank is in "*Cracking the Code on Amazon Sales Rank: Understanding Sales Rank for Maximum Profits*.")

The worse the Sales Rank, the more important condition becomes. When you get worse than 1 million, you really should be aiming to be the next sale by any means necessary, and every detail in your listing counts. *Especially* condition.

"But another buyer will come along eventually…"

Maybe. But maybe not. Most books that sell upwards of $30 are poorly ranked, and aren't getting buyers every day, or even every month. In the aforementioned example of a $75 book on a university press – just those two data points alone (high price + "university press") should indicate to most booksellers that its Sales Rank is well worse than 1 million. So if one buyer is coming along every six months, you better be certain your offer is optimized to get that sale.

That's what this book is for.

About me: How I learned all these cool Jedi tricks

Since 2007, I've sold tens of thousands of books on Amazon. I've seen every form of damaged, defaced, destroyed, disgraced, disintegrated book known to man. And through this nearly decade-long obstacle course of coffee-stains-and-library-stamps, I've learned a lot of tricks. I've gone into antiquarian bookstores and talked to the cool old guys behind the counter to learn their techniques. And I've invented a few of my own.

Over the last several years, three of my best sources have offered entirely, or almost entirely, library books. Here are some stats from one of the three:

- Average yield per month: Over 200 books.
- Average listing price: over $25
- Average Sales Rank: worse than 4 million.
- Average condition: Acceptable.

In fact, almost all of these retired library books were "Acceptable," if that.

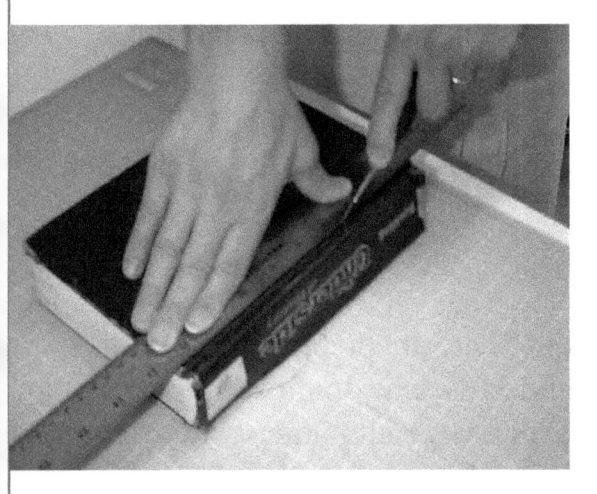

Yes, these stats are pretty bad. And it's books like these where every detail counts, or you'll never get the sale. So I started to set aside the really valuable ones, and perform experiments.

I piled up boxes of books in the $50+ range, to see if I could upgrade them from Acceptable to Good, or Very Good. As I got better, I aimed to erase any hint these were ex-library books at all. And I got pretty good at it.

This book represents everything I've learned, and everything I know about increasing the value of your books and media.

When I use these tricks: My personal formula

Knowing when to dedicate the time to upgrading a book is a calculation based on several variables. Specifically: Time required, value of book, and what condition category we can raise it to.

If a book is selling for $15 and in Good condition, and the best I can hope for is to get it to Very Good, I'm not going to touch it. I'm listing it as Good and moving on. For one, there aren't enough buyers who care about the distinction between Very Good and Good for it to affect the likelihood of a sale that much. If it was a poorly ranked book with low demand, and was priced a little higher, I may take 10 minutes and give it a condition overhaul so that it has a chance of selling, vs. languishing away in my inventory for eternity.

I will *not* take time to increase a book from Good to Very Good condition unless one of the following two conditions applies:

- A book is valuable.
- A book is very poorly ranked.

As for the former, if a book is in medium-bad Sales Rank range, and has moderate-to-high value, I'll take the time to increase it from Good to Very Good because there's significant enough money on the line.

As for the latter, every detail counts when you're in the supra-two-million Sales Rank category. Now, I'm still not spending an hour to repair a $10 book of any rank, but when it will only take a few minutes, I'll make the effort.

Now, what if that same book was in Acceptable condition? I will do almost anything to get a book out of Acceptable. As the lowest condition on Amazon's scale, buyers will pass on your book to buy others. With lower-demand books, having a listing in Acceptable condition is almost like not having it listed as all.

And what if a good is nearly perfect, except for one minor blemish? That deserves it's own section…

We're going to make books new again

The largest price discrepancies exist between Used and New. There are literally millions of books on Amazon that are one penny in used condition, and $10+ new. In most instances, getting a book from used condition to New will translate into 500%+ profit increase, making this type of repair a very valuable skill set.

So, when are we turning books into new?

The conditions in which we can employ this tactic are limited. But when we can, it's profitable. Here are the conditions:

•   Unread books with minor, correctible blemishes. Price marks on the first page, remainder marks, etc.
•   Unread books that have wear that approximates what a book might incur during shipping. (*Customers understand they ordered a book through the mail, and this isn't a book taken right off the shelf.*)
•   Books that may have been read, but remain in virtually new condition.

The book *can't* have any evidence the book has ever been opened. That's the part you can't cut corners on.

Turning used books into New: Where the money is.

Your obligation as an Amazon seller is to meet the needs of the customer. To accomplish, you must meet their expectations and know what they are expecting when they place an order with you. So when a customer buys a New book, what are they buying?

They are buying a cosmetically flawless book that then endured a long journey with the US postal service.

What does this mean?

First of all, have you ever ordered a New book on Amazon? It never arrives in fresh-off-the-press condition. It can arrive close, but never flawless. People understand that a long trip through the mail will result in some slight wear. Even if it's just a small bump to a corner. People get it.

I'm an FBA seller, and in my book Amazon Autopilot I recount the time I ordered a New condition book from myself. What arrived was a book that was very much *not* in New condition. Every corner had some damage, and it looked exactly like a New book that had spent several days in the mail. Which is what it was.

This means that what you put in the envelope (or box to UPS) should be very, very close to flawless.

Note that I said the expectation of a customer is a book in *near-perfect* condition. Not an "unread" book. What's the difference? It is entirely possible to read a book and leave exactly no perceptible evidence you did so. Have you ever purchased a book, read it in one sitting, and put it on your shelf? There's a good chance that if that book never went into your backpack, got thrown around in your car, or was never opened multiple times, there is no evidence it was ever read.

Whether a book is "read" or not is merely an academic distinction. If there is zero perceptible evidence of it having been read, it wasn't read. Because if a tree falls in the forest and no one hears it…

Likewise, if your customer is happy, then you have fulfilled your obligation as a seller. That's it.

Let's go into the subject of what New condition is a little deeper…

The non-negotiable elements of New condition

- No evidence the book has been opened: No creases in the spine. A book that opens like it's for the first time.
- That "new book" sheen. There's a shine to a New book. You don't even have to touch a book for that shine to disappear over time. (*We're going to show you how to restore it like it never left.*)
- Absolutely no blemishes inside. Any sign that the book has been opened, and you can't list it as New.

How to get ten times the profit for minimal work

It is completely normal (and generally true) that books in New condition bring 300%+ more than their used counterparts. Most often, they will bring literally *10 times* the profit.

Here's why:

The majority of used books on Amazon are listed for a penny. It didn't used to be this way, but the glut of sellers into the space has made it so. Whether you sell Merchant Fulfilled or via Fulfillment by Amazon, you're bringing in somewhere in the range of 40 cents per penny book when all the smoke clears.

Now let's look at that same book in New condition. There is no public data on this to draw from, but I would estimate the average New book is selling for $8. Maybe it's $15, maybe its $5. Let's just go with $8. How much profit you're left with depends on how you sell (merchant fulfilled vs. FBA), but let's just assume you're taking home $4 on average from a book in New condition (it's probably higher).

Thusly, by raising a book from used to new condition, you are on average increasing its value 10x.

Enter your nagging grandmother

There are petty people who throw temper tantrums over these techniques, but I'm pretty sure they aren't smart enough to understand what the term "cosmetically flawless" means. We've already lost them. This is for the rest of you.

The highest priority should be placed on delivering a satisfactory experience for the customer. It's good for your feedback score, and good in general. In the simplest terms, this means giving the customer exactly what they're paying for – and exactly what they expect. This is your obligation as a seller, and this obligation trumps everything.

(Sidebar: You know how there's one crazy person at the front of every bus who talks to the driver? There is one crazy person in every internet forum who like to complain about everything. They'll even declare there is something morally questionable about listing a cosmetically flawless [in other words: New] book as "New." Of course they'll never explain themselves, because obviously, that's the dumbest thing in the world. If you want to know what these people sound like, check out Ted Knight's wife in Caddyshack.)

If a book is in new condition, it's a new book. If a buyer orders a new book and receives (surprise) a new book in new condition, you've delivered on your promise and should be commended as an Amazon seller.

The only detail that makes a cosmetically flawless book not

new is the academic detail that it has a previous owner. That's it.

The special case of textbooks

Oh, and then there's textbooks. The ones with very subtle wear are the perfect candidates for the Like-New-to-New conversion. My experience has taught that we can relax our standards slightly with textbooks. The intentions behind a textbook buyer selecting a "New" copy are somewhat different than the average book buyer. Specifically, students are paying for two things:

- The guaranteed absence of highlighting and writing.
- The guaranteed presence of all inserts, unused access codes, etc.

The presence of a light (*light*) amount of "shelving wear" is less of a concern to textbook buyers than the aforementioned two things. Textbooks are almost never purchased as gifts, so we can cross off the majority of concerns that usually go along with shipping a "New" book through the mail. Textbook buyers don't want a trophy. They just want a book that is new in the ways that matter: No highlighting, and all inserts included.

With all other books, greater strictness must be maintained.

A note on Very Good vs. Good

I've watched this subject closely, and I can say that buyers do not have a strong preference for books in Very Good condition over Good. To most Amazon buyers, it all translates to "average used copy." As such, I'll only take the time to improve the condition of a book in Good condition if certain conditions apply (see: "*When I use these tricks: My personal formula.*")

Where this upgrade does matter is in how Amazon sorts listings. Your feedback score and the condition of the offer are the two factors Amazon looks at to determine who gets the top spot (besides price, obviously). So this might matter more than you'd think.

And it's even more important if you're selling to a collector. Which brings us to…

The difference between books that appeal to Collectors, and those that appeal to everyone else

Most collectors won't touch a book in Good condition.

This distinction affects your willingness to do more time-intensive condition hacks, and how far you should go. The distinction comes from understanding who your book is selling to.

More specifically, if they are a "collector" or "general buyer."

Doing the "collector / non-collector" math is irrelevant if you're dealing with a book in the $25 and under range. This is left to personal priorities of course, but I give a lot of attention to this question in this range, personally. You should be much more focused on getting massive amounts of new inventory that hovering over a $25 book with an iron for an hour, trying to remove the library pocket from the inside cover.

When you get north of that, it might be time to consider putting some serious time into the book. The first question to ask is: Who is your buyer?

To answer that, we have to distinguish between Collectors and General Buyers. If your book will only sell to Collectors, there are a few things you have to know:

- Few will buy books that aren't in VG condition or better.
- Details are everything, and every blemish counts to this crowd.
- You shouldn't be listing the book on Amazon.

If you have a book that only appeals to collectors, every detail matters in terms of making the sale. To the extent that the projected profit is worth your time, you should spare no details in optimizing your books condition for the collector market. To collectors, details *matter*... a lot.

I sell very, very few books I would classify as collectible. Many sellers *only* sell collectible books. I have just enough high-end collectible books to maintain an Abe Books account, but barely.

Collectors are just not buying on Amazon. Here are where they are:

- AbeBooks.com ($25 a month.)
- Alibris.com ($20 a year.)
- Ebay.com (Small fee + commission.)

Condition is everything when selling to the collector's market. *Everything*.

If you're used to selling on Amazon, you're in for a sobering experience when you start selling to the collector market. Your inventory isn't going to turn over nearly as much. And not at all if you aren't addressing your book's blemishes, and fixing them.

Online, most collectors shop at Abe. If you have enough books to justify the $300 / year fees, go with them. If not, I would bypass Alibris and go straight for eBay. Only if you have very few collectible books yet are 100% committed to getting top dollar for them would I advise going with Alibris.

The recipe for determining what is collectible is subtle. "Old" is not the only factor. This subject is outside the scope of this book, but it's important that you *know your customer*. If your book only has appeal to collectors, it's probably not selling on Amazon. And you better get that book into VG+ territory or it's not selling.

Here are Amazon's condition guidelines

You need to memorize these. This are the guidelines, straight from Amazon's mouth:

- *New*: Just like it sounds. A brand-new, unused, unread copy in perfect condition. The dust cover and original protective wrapping, if any, are intact. All supplementary materials are included and all access codes for electronic material, if applicable, are valid and/or in working condition.
- *Used - Like New*: Dust cover is intact, with no nicks or tears. Spine has no signs of creasing. Pages are clean and not marred by notes or folds of any kind. May contain remainder marks on outside edges, which should be noted in listing comments.
- *Used - Very Good*: Pages and dust cover are intact and not marred by notes or highlighting. The spine is undamaged.
- *Used - Good*: All pages and cover are intact (including the dust cover, if applicable). Spine may show signs of wear. Pages may include limited notes and highlighting. May include "From the library of" labels.
- *Used - Acceptable*: All pages and the cover are intact, but the dust cover may be missing. Pages may include limited notes and highlighting, but the text cannot be obscured or unreadable.
- *Unacceptable*: Includes missing pages and obscured or unreadable text. We also do not permit the sale of advance reading copies, including uncorrected proofs, of in-print or not-yet-published books.

The benefit of grading conservatively

The vast, vast majority of negative feedback you will receive will come from customers disputing your choice of condition among the used categories. In my years as an Amazon seller, I have received almost no negative feedback for New books a customer felt weren't New.

Most negative feedback will come from customers arguing that a book in VG condition should have been G, a book in G condition should have been Acceptable, or Acceptable books that people didn't read the condition description for and left bad feedback anyway.

Throughout this book, keep in mind my advice: *Grade conservatively.* Under-promise and over-deliver.

How this book is divided

Each of these tricks is primarily suited for one of three categories:

1. Turning Very Good books into New.
2. Turning Acceptable books into Good or better.
3. Turning Good books into Very Good.

They are sorted in the order of profitability, with the biggest value increase to be had in the leap from used condition to new (i.e. the first one).

The second is from Acceptable to Good (or better). Acceptable condition books can be very slow to move unless they are in high demand, and these tricks can turn a book that will never sell into one that will.

Lastly, taking a Good condition book and turning into Very Good (or even Like New). If your book's price matches that over other sellers, this can tip the scales and make your offer the top listing and the next sale.

When to hire a professional

There are two times to hire a professional book restoration expert:

1. Any book that has major, major, *major* value.
2. A book with significant value that might incur permanent damage if you employ a complicated restoration tactic and it goes wrong.

This will not be a situation that most booksellers ever encounter. Most people whose business is entirely on Amazon aren't dealing with books on this level. But should a book like this fall into your hands, you should be aware there are professionals who can be called in to help.

Bonus: Several tricks for increasing the value of books + condition hacking other media

If you're selling books, you're probably selling other used media. I have you covered.

I'm throwing a couple techniques to increase the value of your books, and a couple more for

DVDs & CDs. These tricks can turn items that are literally worthless and unsellable into cash.

These small tricks are the reasons I don't hesitate to buy scuffed CDs and DVDs, incomplete sets, and more. These are straightforward and simple tactics that will make you money.

Your condition hacking toolbox

If you're a serious bookseller, you may want to go out and pick most of these things up to stock your book repair toolbox. Or you can just acquire them as-needed.

There are a few "book repair kits" being sold online in the $50+ range, but they are mostly everyday items assembled together and marked up. You don't need one of these.

This is the list of every took I mention in this entire book:

- Mars Staedtler plastic eraser or Magic Rub eraser
- Scotty Peeler Label & Sticker Remover (*Pay a little more and get the $9 set with the metal peeler. This kit will be recommended in at least 10 of the fixes I'm covering in this book. Available on Amazon.*)
- WD-40
- Rubbing alcohol
- Cotton swab
- Cotton cloth
- Nail polish remover
- X-acto knife
- Pencil
- Scissors
- Vaseline
- Stickers
- 100-grip and 320-grip sandpaper
- Mineral spirits, naphtha, or turpentine
- Goo Gone or rubber cement thinner (Heptane)
- Paper towels
- Quilting iron / standard iron
- Wax paper
- Large Zip lock bags

Disclaimer

Many of these tricks call for bending (or snapping in half) Amazon's rules governing condition. For example, I have listed easily hundreds of books from which I have removed damaged yet blank pages, though this is technically not consistent with the letter of Amazon's law.

I have two immutable rules when I decide to bend Amazon's policies:

1. I am not advocating anything that cheats or otherwise deprives the customer of any value.
2. I am not advising anything for which I have ever received negative feedback. Ever.

One note: Any trick here that calls for bending Amazon's rules should not be applied to a collectible book that will sell to a collector. The collector will notice. And they will not be forgiving.

- Medical bandage
- PVA (Polyvinyl acetate) adhesive
- Bulldog clip
- Squares of cardboard
- Clean Cover Gel
- Smelleze® Reusable Book and Antique Deodorizer Pou
or- book deodorizer –or- essential oils –or- fabric softener sh
- Book dust jacket replacement covers set
- Paint brush
- Three-ring binders
- Lacquer-removing solvent
- Lifting knife

Erasers
When repairing books, you'll be taking erasers to everything from library stamps to notes in the margins. Here are your options:

Vinyl
The best all-purpose erasers. Pros: They are softer and less abrasive, making them less likely to do damage. Con: The firmer varieties are more prone to smearing and smudging.

Gum
The best eraser for "smudges" (vs. ink, etc).

Rubber
These are functional, but lower-grade and prone to smearing. Will do the job for many fixes.

Electric erasers
These don't allow for the greatest precision, but this can shave a lot of time off a large erasing job.

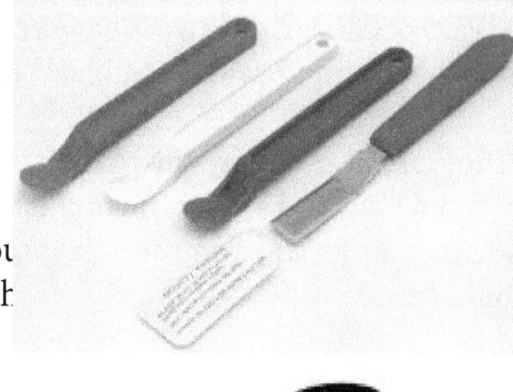

How to use this book

Pay only minimal attention to what chapter each blemish is in. The best way to read this book is to scan the Table of Contents for the particular blemish you're dealing with, rather than by the book's current condition.

The chapters are headed by what condition a book can be upgraded to if only one of the conditions apply. If two or more of the conditions apply, you may have a harder time upgrading a book from VG to N, or G to VG.

For example, some type of Sharpie marks on covers or spines are common. If that's the only blemish a book has suffered, then it can be upgraded to New through application of the fix described.

If, however, a book has been retired from a library, you can rescue this book from Acceptable condition, but it will never be restored to New.

If you have any damaged book, no matter it's current condition, you should scan the entire table of contents until you find it.

Let's get into it.

Flippant disclaimer:

I have never received negative feedback for anything I'm describing here in tens of thousands of transactions. If my advice results in another experience, you have permission to sue.

Section II

How to restore a book to New condition. If you have a book that is New except for one of these blemishes – here's how to fix them.

How to fix books with...
A remainder mark or other ink on cover
A dirty or dusty exterior
An irremovable blemish on a blank or unnecessary page:
A price written in the corner of the first page.
A damaged dust jacket.
Ink in the corner of a title page (e.g. price marked in pen, owner's name, etc)
Writing or ink on one or more pages
A cover that has lost its shine
A stain or blemish on the back cover
A fold to the corner of a page
A remainder mark

How to restore a book to New condition. If you have a book that is New except for one of these blemishes – here's how to fix them.

Problem: Sharpie mark on cover / other ink on a cover.

Example: I have one source that writes the price in Sharpie on every book cover. It's quite obnoxious, but I apply this fix and have restored many books to New condition.

Solution: My personal quick fix solution is WD-40, applied with a soft cloth, tissue, or cotton ball. It's pure magic how quickly and efficiently it will remove ink from glossy-paper surfaces. Regular isopropyl alcohol or nail polish remover will serve a similar purpose.

Apply very lightly. A little will go a long way. Too much will have two adverse effects. One, it may stain the paper. Two, the smell will devalue the book and offend the purchaser. Apply conservatively. It doesn't take much.

Only apply to glossy dust jackets or glossy softcovers. Can stain anything else.

Problem: A book with a dirty or dusty exterior.

Example: You have an otherwise New book that has been stored improperly and has accumulated dust or other grime.

Solution #1: For a glossy cover, wipe down the book with a dusting cloth.

Solution #2: For a cloth cover, use Clean Cover Gel. This is not water based, and will not harm the cloth or cause it to run. Can also be used on soft covers.

Solution #3: For glossy dust jackets, wipe down with a solution of 50% water and 50% Windex. Apply the Windex to the rag, not directly to the book. Pretty simple.

Problem: An irremovable blemish on a blank or unnecessary page:

Example: You find a book in New condition, that was given as a gift, has a gift inscription ("Happy birthday Ryan!"), and was never read.

Solution: This one is dangerous, but can restore a book to new condition if done properly. It takes delicate care and some degree of luck.

If there are any marks or stains on a *blank or unnecessary page* (redundant title page, etc), then you might have an option.

With frequent but inconsistent success, I have taken an X-acto knife and very, very carefully cut out the page as close to the spine as possible. If done very well, this can be almost imperceptible.

If not done well, you are begging for bad feedback. Use very cautiously, and do extremely well or not at all.

Unnecessary disclaimer: I shouldn't have to tell you this, but you should never remove a page that has any non-redundant content whatsoever. This is about improving the condition of a book, not depriving customers of value.

Problem: Price written in corner of first page.

Example: One of my biggest sources is a bookstore inside of a library. They pencil a price inside every single book, in the corner of the first page. Many of these books are flawless, brand new books – except for this writing.

This is common in many environments, from thrift stores to used bookstores.

Solution #1: Erase the writing.

Even pen may be erasable, so it's worth attempting to remove the writing entirely with an eraser. Whether pencil or erasable pen, this can often be done to the point it is imperceptible.

Solution #2: If the writing cannot be erased, here's a trick I use often.

A lot of the books I purchase at the aforementioned source are 50 cents, written as ".50." I will first take note of the new, cover price of the book. I will then take a pencil or pen (of the same color) and pencil in a number or numbers just in front of the ".50" that will bring the total figure to within 50 cents of the cover price. For example, if the cover price of a book is $15, I'll write a "15" in front of the ".50", so that it appears wherever it came was selling it as a New copy, for $15.50.

If a customer sees "50 cents" written inside a "new"

book, they'll think you got something over on them. If they see "$15.50" inside a New book they paid $7 for, they think they got one over on you.

In the case of books you'll list as used, is also generally advisable to remove or alter any price written inside if that price is less than you intend to sell it for on Amazon. Some highly-sensitive buyers may be offended to receive a book they paid $7 for, that they see you paid $1 for.

Problem: A book with a damaged dust jacket.

Example: You acquire a book with a tear in the dust jacket, that has a flawlessly New book underneath.

Solution: I cover damage dust jackets in a later chapter as well, so look there if this entry doesn't' apply to your situation. This is a trick that can be applied in a very specific situation, with a specific kind of book.

Increasingly, books are being printed that have the same artwork actually printed on to the paperboard cover itself as is on the jacket. You'll see this with fiction most often, but you'll see this with all genres from time to time.

If you have such a book, you can remove the dust jacket and throw it away. What's left is essentially the exact same book, with the same artwork.

I've done this many times. And there's a 99% chance the buyer doesn't even know the book ever had a dust jacket. And if they do, there's a 99% chance they don't care. Why should they?

Problem: Ink in the corner of a title page

Example: You purchased an otherwise New book at a library sale, with a price marked in pen in the corner of the first page.

Solution: Cut the corner off.

For this trick you're exploiting a common practice called a "price clip." This is a routine alteration made to remainder or overstock hardcover books. It consists of a corner of the dust jacket flap being cut. This serves the same function as a remainder mark, denoting a book as having been marked down and sold in a bargain bin. Generally, this is done to hardcover books only, but I get a little loose with tradition for this trick…

I snip the corner off with scissors and in the description note: "Price clip on title page." The stats don't lie; I've never gotten negative feedback for this. While this disfigurement is generally only made to a dust jacket, I just extend the definition by one page. No harm, no foul.

Problem: Writing or ink on one or more pages

Example: Someone writes notes on two pages of a textbook.

Solution: This becomes more difficult when writing is abundant, but I have had great success erasing pencil or erasable pen completely, leaving no trace it was ever there.

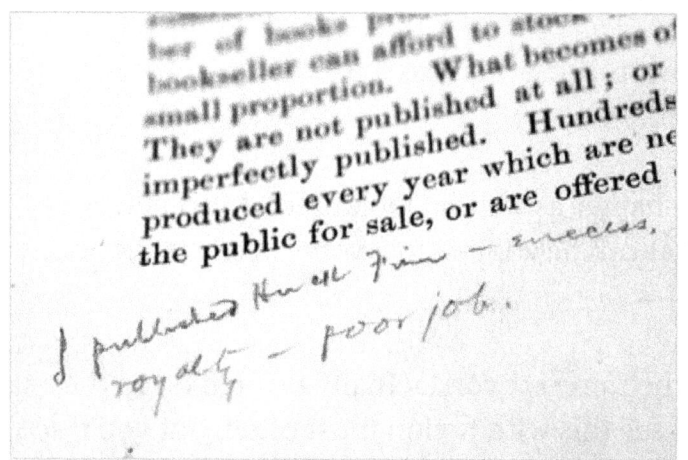

This is where we get schooled in the bizarre and boring science of erasers. There are many kinds of erasers. And there are many kinds of ink. And sometimes the right eraser on the right ink can destroy it. That's what we want.

There are many times when you have an otherwise New book with writing on a few pages, or a stamp of some sort, and it seems hopeless. But it might not be.

First, get a Sanford Mars Staedtler plastic eraser. Designed for artists, these are gentle on the page and you can know if it's working before doing any damage. These are the standard for removing ink from paper. But they have their limits. A lot of limits.

When the value of a book is high enough, I have spent an hour erasing a page or more of pen marks or underlining. Consider the value of your time, but especially in the case of textbooks, it can definitely be worth the time.

The trick of course is to remove the writing completely and fully if you intend to list a book as New. This can be either simple or difficult, depending on the type of writing instrument used, but it can be done.

In cases where a book cannot be listed as new, erasing a significant amount of writing can raise a book from Acceptable to Good or Very Good.

Problem: Restoring a "new book shine" to a book's cover

Example: You have a New book that has been removed from a shelf repeatedly and lost its shine.

Solution: Do a once-over with rubbing alcohol and a rag, then give a light application of Vaseline; a dab of it on a soft clean cloth can restore shine to dust jackets. Wipe it on and wipe it off.

Problem: A stain or blemish on the back cover.

Example: You have a textbook with a irremovable price tag on the back cover.

Solution: FBA sellers have a huge advantage here. All FBA offers are required to have a roughly 2" x 3.5" sticker on the back, over the barcode. It's supposed to go over the barcode. In the event there is a blemish somewhere that is not the barcode, I will bend the rules and place the sticker over the blemish. Problem solved.

If you're not an FBA seller, you can still apply this tactic. It may take some work, but you can format and print a label (using a sheet of labels in your printer, or a label printer if you have one) and place over the blemish. A standard FBA will have a barcode, along with the title of the book and its condition. What's important is that the label looks like it belongs and serves a function, and wasn't put there just to cover up an imperfection.

Problem: A fold to the corner of a page.

Example: You acquire a book in otherwise New condition, that has the corner of a page folded over as a bookmark.

Solution: First, slide a piece of firm card stock under the bent page.

Then cover the page with a piece of paper to protect from overheating.

Then run clothes or quilting iron over the fold.

If the crease is not too severe, this can erase evidence of a fold entirely.

If this doesn't work, put a small, small, small amount of water on the tip of a cotton swab and dab a minute amount of water along the fold. This will cause the fibers of the paper to swell. Then iron again.

Problem: Remainder marks

Example: You acquire a New book from an overstock store that has a pen mark along the book's fore-edge (aka a remainder mark).

Solution: When I learned about this, something close to "Hallelujah" came out of my mouth. This is an extremely common problem that I was ecstatic about finding a solution for.

A little primer on remainder marks: Generally, these consist of a black marker being swabbed across the "fore-edge" of the book (the three edges of the pages you see when you turn any book 90 degrees from the cover). This indicates a book has been downgraded from being a "cover price" item, and sold at a discount. For example, if you check out the bargain bin at most bookstores that sell new books, you'll find the books have remainder marks.

According to Amazon's policies, an unread book with a remainder mark can only be sold in Like New condition. However you will see a ton of large Amazon sellers listing these books as new, with the condition note reading "May have remainder mark." I did this myself for a long time. Until I learned this trick.

Take small piece of 100-grip sandpaper. Take the adhesive side and put it against your pointer finger. In the case of a hardcover, be sure that you cut or tear the sandpaper so it does not rub against the covers of the book. Rub your finger against the remainder mark repeatedly, and you will see the ink mark start to vanish almost instantly. In 30 seconds or so, you will see it vanish altogether.

You just turned a Like New (i.e. "used") book into a New one.

Section III

How to upgrade a book to Good (or Very Good) condition. If you have a book that is Acceptable because of a defect listed here – your solution has arrived.

How to fix books with…
A tilted spine.
A severely split or feathered corner or corners (most effective with hardcovers)
A curved cover of hardcover book
A reeeeally bad smell
An extremely torn or damaged dust jacket.
A smudge mark on the cover of a cloth hardcover book.
Highlighting

How to upgrade a book to Good (or Very Good) condition. If you have a book that is Acceptable because of a defect listed here – your solution has arrived.

Problem: Tilted spine

Example: You have a book that has spent a lot of time under major weight and has suffered a cocked spine.

Solution: Re-align the book by hand, then wrap tightly with a fabric medical bandage, then place under a heavy object (such as other books) for a few days or weeks. The book should be re-squared to its original glory.

Problem: Severely split or feathered corners (most effective with hardcovers).

Example: You acquire a hardcover book in average used condition, except for trauma to a corner resulting in a split.

Solution: Use a paint brush or micro-spatula and apply a small amount of diluted PVA into the feathered corner. Get in between as many layers of the feathered paper as you can. Apply pressure and push the feathered corner flat. Remove excess PVA with a cloth or paper towel. Cover the corner with wax paper, then sandwich between small pieces of cardboard. Hold it all together with a bulldog clip. Leave overnight, and then remove.

Don't be afraid to do more damage to the book than already exists. Doing this process properly may involve actually pulling apart the cover to get the PVA deeper inside to do a thorough repair.

Problem: Curved cover of hardcover book

Example: A book has been stored under pressure, resulting in a bent spine that does not sit evenly against the pages.

Solution: Remove the dust jacket. Put a damp paper towel flat against the inside cover. Place a piece of wax paper or plastic between the paper towel and the pages. Put the book under a lot of weight. Leave there for several days.

Check the book, and repeat until the cover lays flat against the interior.

Problem: Books that smell really bad

Example: A book that has mildewed after being stored in a moist environment.

Books that smell very bad for whatever reason can often be completely unsellable. These tactics will remove (or mask) the offensive smell.

Solution #1: Place the book in an airtight zip lock bag with a single piece of charcoal. Leave the book there for two weeks. The charcoal will slowly absorb the smell over that time. Check the book after two weeks, and leave longer if needed.

Solution #2: Put the book in a sealed zip lock bag with unscented cat litter. Also leave for two weeks. Repeat if needed.

Solution #3: Put the book, again, in a sealed bag with a substance called Book Deodorizer. Yes, that's its name. It is made just for these occasions, and can be purchased online.

Solution #4: Put the book in Smelleze® Reusable Book and Antique Deodorizer Pouch. Another tool made just for these occasions. And can also be purchased for $15 on Amazon. Here is the description, from the manufacturer:

"One of the problems encountered in old books is the harmful result of exposure to moisture over a long period of time. Humid conditions promote the growth of mold and mildew which results in books having a musty odor. Smoke and other odors can also be absorbed by books over time and result in unpleasant book odors. Some collectors are very sensitive about book odors and this could negatively affect their value. The Smelleze® Book Deodorizer Pouch was specially developed to eliminate musty odors from all types of old books, magazines, papers, antiques and other unwashable objects without harming them. It works by effectively absorbing and encapsulating phenomenal amounts of musty and other book odors without masking them with fragrances. For a breathe of fresh air, simply place a reusable Smelleze® pouch with up to 12 books in an airtight plastic bag, plastic container or cooler for about a week or until the odors are eliminated. Books, magazines, documents, antiques and other unwashable items may also be stored with Smelleze® over long periods of time to absorb moisture and to prevent musty mold and mildew odors permeating them."

Solution #5: Use a strong essential oil. Add drops of an essential oil like lavender, eucalyptus or tea-tree oil to some cotton balls. Place in a resealable plastic bag. Add the book and seal. Remove after a few days; you should find the book smells more like the essential oil than whatever it smelled like before. Because of the risk of oil spots, only do this with books that don't have great value other than needing to be read, such as a moldy-but-useful textbook.

Solution #6: Cut a bunch of fabric softener sheets into thirds, and put one between every 20 pages or so in your smelly book. Keep it in a zipper bag for a few days, and the musty smell should be gone.

Problem: A book with an extremely torn and damaged dust jacket

Example: A hardcover book that has a large chunk of the dust jacket torn away.

Solution #1: Buy a blank replacement cover.

A very damaged dust jacket will always equal "Acceptable condition". So you have to start by getting rid of the offensive dust jacket.

This trick is not, of course, an equal replacement of the original. But an extremely damaged dust jacket is worse than none at all. And a nice, shiny, new plastic slipcover is better than both. These are available in various sizes on Amazon, and can be cut to size if you have an oddly shaped book. It's interesting how much the perceived value of a book is increased by slipping a shiny new dust jacket on it.

Solution #2: Just throw the dust jacket away and sell without the cover.

Problem: Smudge marks on the cover of a cloth hardcover book

Example: A book that has a large smudge on a cover-less hardcover.

Solution: Get a Mars Staedtler plastic eraser. This will completely lift most smudges or blemishes on cloth hardcovers.

If the eraser lightens the fabric noticeably, take eraser and go over the area around the former stain lightly to even out the color.

Problem: Highlighting on pages

Example: You have a textbook a student has highlighted on many pages.

Solution: I have to give a huuuuge disclaimer here. I almost included this in a section of "things you can't do anything about," because I assumed if it was possible my research would have turned it up before. But I looked into it a little more, and found someone who claimed to have a solution.

According to the source, this will remove yellow highlighting only. And it may leave behind a slight blue-yellow tint.

With the understanding that I have not tried this, here's their solution for removing highlighting:

1. Pour lemon juice into a small bowl or cup.
2. Have an electric or hand-operated fan ready to help it dry faster. The faster it dries, the less wrinkling of the paper
3. Take a Q-tip cotton swab and dip the tip of it only into the lemon juice. Get merely damp – less is more.
4. Lightly run the tip over the ink. If there's no significant damage to the paper, then continue lightly swabbing in horizontal lines following the direction of the markings until the color almost disappears.
5. When you are done swabbing two side-by-side pages, leave them open for 1-2 minutes to allow them to dry before you proceed to the next pages

Section IV

How to upgrade a book to Very Good condition. If you have a book that is merely Good – here's how to get it up to Very Good.

How to fix books with...
A grease stain on a cloth cover.
Pages marked with White Out
Stickers or sticker residue on the front or back cover.
A book plate on the inside cover or one of the first pages.
A dust jacket that has wrinkles, folds, or waves

How to upgrade a book to Very Good condition. If you have a book that is merely Good – here's how to get it up to Very Good.

Problem: Grease stain on a cloth cover.

Example: Your book has greasy fingerprints from a previous owner.

Solution: Dry-cleaning fluid or non-water based spot remover works well on most food or grease stains. Not to be used on soft covers.

Problem: Pages with White Out

Example: A book with pen marks that a previous owner attempted to remedy with correction fluid.

Solution: A small amount of White Out should not degrade a book to the level of Acceptable, but a lot of White Out will. In either case, there is a simple remedy.

Mineral spirits, naphtha, and turpentine (all found in the paint section of a hardware store) will re-liquefy White Out. Apply the solvent to the White Out, then dab away the White Out with a cosmetic round or rag.

Problem: Stickers or sticker residue on the front or back cover

Example: A book from a retail setting blemished with a hard-to-remove price sticker.

Solution: Many solutions will remove stickers.

This is a very common problem remedied by a solution called Goo Gone. Get some. Use in conjunction with the Scotty Peeler Label & Sticker Remover (available on Amazon) These are perfect for removing labels from books. Worth the investment.

As alternatives to Goo Gone, mineral spirits, naphtha, and Heptane (sold as rubber cement thinner) work well to remove stickers.

Problem: A book plate on the inside cover or one of the first pages

Example: You acquire a collection of books from a personal library, each of which has the owners personal book plate pasted to the inside cover.

Solution: Book plates are usually adhered by the original purchaser to denote ownership. They are also often used by libraries. They may say something like "*From the library of…*"

There are two types of book plates: Those adhered with glue, and those affixed with standard sticker adhesive. Rule of thumb: If they are glossy, they're stickers. If not, assume glue.

Glossy plates: Use a standard iron or quilting iron on low heat until the book plate starts to loosen. You may want to iron through a sheet of paper, but this is not always necessary. Use a Scotty Peeler or spatula to ease up the edges of the book plate as it heats, working your way to the middle until it lifts off completely.

Glue-adhered plates: Cut a paper towel down to the size of book plate. Squeeze out the excess water until it is merely "damp." Water will re-activate the glue.

If the book plate is on a page (rather than the inside cover), you will want to place some barrier on the opposite side of the page to prevent moisture from reaching additional pages. A zip lock bag is sufficient.

Cover the paper towel with something water-proof like another plastic bag or wax paper. Close the book, put under something heavy, and wait 30 minutes to an hour.

The book plate should then be sufficiently loose enough to begin easing up with a Scotty Peeler or spatula. Repeat as needed.

When removed, iron to dry, place page in direct sunlight, or leave open in a warm dry place to prevent warping of the damp spot.

Problem: A dust jacket with wrinkles, folds, or waves

Example: A book whose cover suffered a light amount of water damage.

Solution: Take the dust jacket off the book and lay it face down on a heat-proof surface (like a counter). Lay a thin towel over it. Iron on low. Let it sit for several minutes to cool before removing from the surface.

For folds, use an iron with a small surface so that you can more accurately direct the heat, such as a quilting iron.

Section V

How to turn a damaged, unsellable book into one you can turn into money.

How to fix books with…
A cover or back cover that reads "Promotional Copy Only – Not for Sale."
A page torn out
A batch of pages that have been torn out
Water damage
Major damage that is literally falling apart, has a cover torn off, or has other massive structural damage

How to turn a damaged, unsellable book into one you can turn into money.

Problem: A book is marked as "Promotional Copy Only – Not for Sale."

Example: You acquire a new textbook that was distributed free to professors for promotional purposes.

Solution: This is most often seen with promotional copies of textbooks, sent to universities. Promotional copies of non-textbooks generally have completely different artwork than their non-promotional counterparts. With textbooks, often the artwork is identical, save for a small box on the back cover describing it a promotional copy.

A warning, before doing this: Confirm that the contents of the book are the same as a non-promotional copy. Thumb through to verify there isn't anything inside that reveals it as a promotional copy.

If it passes this test, you can place an FBA or FBA-similar sticker (with the book name, condition, and barcode) over the "not for sale" artwork. You can also get creative, and cover the artwork with another sticker of your own choosing. What matters is that the sticker appears to have a legitimate purpose, and isn't placed there just to cover something.

If you follow these guidelines, this is will turn an unsellable textbook into a sellable one.

Problem: The book has a page torn out, but the page has been retained

Example: You purchased a used textbook, with a torn page that was folded up and slipped back in the pages. (That happens more often than you'd think.)

Solution: When you still have the page, you can do some surgery to remedy this.

A book missing a (non-blank) page can't – and shouldn't – be sold. That's number one.

Obtain some PVA, or polyvinyl acetate. Open the book to where the page should be. Using a small paint brush, apply a minute amount of PVA along the 'gutter edge", or the part very close to where the page meets the binding. Apply very lightly. Reinsert the page. Close the book and leave overnight.

Problem: A batch of pages has been torn out of a book

Example: A test-preparation book with perforated, tear-out pages, where a chunk of pages were removed but have been preserved.

Solution: Take the batch of pages, line them up, and secure with spring clips. Take a paint brush and apply a light amount of PVA along the "spine" of this batch. Let dry, and then apply another light layer of PVA to the spine again. Reinsert pages into the book. Close and leave overnight.

Problem: A book got wet and is still wet currently

Example: I used to drive a truck, and more times than I can count I had boxes or bags of books in the back when it started to rain.

Solution: This only works if a book is freshly wet and has not dried.

Absorb as much of the water off the book as possible. Place paper towels between the wet pages and place under weight.

Then stand the book upright and evenly fan out the pages. Place in sunlight if possible and allow the pages to dry. The more quickly a book dries the less page-rippling the book will suffer.

A cover of a hardcover book can also warp from water. Placing the cover in a book press for several days should restore flatness to the cover.

A book that gets wet and allowed to dry is not likely to be a sellable book. Even if you make clear that a book has water damage and is listed as Acceptable, it is at high risk for provoking negative feedback. I've had this happen several times before I learned my lesson.

If a book is dealt with immediately, you can eliminate most of the rippling cause by moisture.

Problem: An 8.5" x 11" (or slightly larger) book that has literally fallen apart, has a cover torn off, or has other massive structural damage

Example: The spine of a textbook has come apart, and the book is literally in pieces.

Solution: This is bound to be the most controversial tactic in the book, so a caveat before we get started: This should only be applied when a book is valuable enough to make it worth both the time and (remote) risk of negative feedback.

Another one: I strongly advise this only be applied to textbooks, or in extreme cases other "instructional," how-to books. Applying this to literature or general non-fiction is not advised, because the repackaging I'm suggesting is less likely to be considered normal and acceptable in other genres.

I promised I would offer you ever emergency measure I've ever used, and this is a weird one. Proceed with caution.

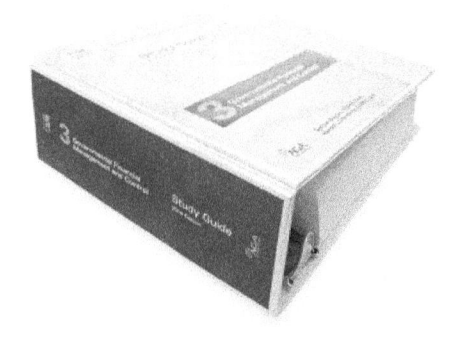

I got this idea when I came upon a large stash of valuable textbooks at a thrift store one day. The only catch was that each of them had been re-binded in three-ring binders. It was all done with surgical precision, with great care taken to put a three hole punch through all the pages, and the cover removed and slid into the clear plastic pouch in the front of the binder. From a production standpoint, it was fairly impressive. Although I had no idea whey someone went to this trouble with over a dozen textbooks.

Most of these reformatted textbooks were selling on Amazon for $20 and up (but costing me 41), and I was confronted with a unique dilemma. Should I list these books? I decided to risk it. I listed them all as Acceptable to weed out picky buyers, and listed the unique binder-format first thing in the condition description. I knew from experience that textbook buyers were much less sensitive to imperfections than other buyers, so I just went for it. No negative feedback resulted.

The next time I found a textbook with a corrupt spine (as in, it was falling apart), I thought of this binder technique. It was an $80 book (if I remember right), so it was worth my time to dissect and reassemble. It was a project, but I got the book into the binder and sold it in Acceptable condition for a fine profit. I've repeated this many times since.

I would detail all the surgical methods that might go into this, but it all depends on what kind of book you're starting with. Generally, it involves removing the cover, removing the pages from the spine, using a paper-cutter along the spine-end of the pages to make them even, hole-punching everything, and sliding the original cover into the front of the binder.

This works best with soft covers, but I've put hardcover-covers into binders as well.

Although you're not depriving a customer of any value, you do run a risk of an unsatisfied customer here. So be warned. Personally, I only apply this technique to textbooks in the $30+ range. A high-risk (but high-profit) condition hack.

Section VI

The science of library book repair: With these tricks, no one will know your book came from a library.

How to fix books with…
A library call number written on the spine
A ton of library stickers and stamps on a plastic slipcover
A library pocket
A library book plate on the inside cover or first page
A library ink stamp inside
A library bar code sticker or other stickers

The science of library book repair: With these tricks, no one will know your book came from a library

If you're dealing in used books, it's inevitable: you're dealing with a lot of retired library books.

Most of what's in this book I learned from dealing with ex-library books. Three of my biggest sources offer either a large percentage of library books, or *all* library books.

Library books are a weird thing. What condition do we list library books under? According to Amazon, books with "library stamps" should be listed as Good condition. But "library stamps" is pretty vague.

Because my policy is to always grade conservatively, if a book has more than just a cople of "library stamps," I often list these as Acceptable. Most library books have at least 4 forms of blemish, from manila pockets, to stamps, to stickers on the spine, and more. More damage than most buyers expect out of a used book, so I'm going conservative.

Also note many (hardcover) library books are missing their original dust jackets. According to Amazon, this is instant Acceptable status. Though I don't personally adhere to this in most cases, when it comes to a library book without a dust jacket, I list it as Acceptable every time.

There are still quite a few ex-library books that are safely in the Good category, and aren't too worse for the wear for having done a tour in a library system. It's a subjective judgment call you have to make.

You really want to state upfront in your condition description that you are selling an "Ex-library book." I remember the time I received negative feedback for someone who accused me of stealing a book from a library, and I was never able to convince her it is totally normal for libraries to retire books and sell them.

The intention of this section is to raise a library book from Acceptable to Good or Very Good, or raise a Good book to Very Good. It's not always possible, but when there is decent money at stake it can be worth the effort.

It is also the intention of this section to, whenever possible, erase any evidence the book came from a library.

Library books are especially important to repair for two reasons:

- Most of the ex-library books I deal in are poorly-ranked, and they might not sell were they not raised from Acceptable condition.
- People see "Ex-library" and are likely to move on to another offer.

Let's look at all the ways library books are altered and/or damaged:

- Library call #s written on spine
- Plastic slip cover
- Library pocket
- Book plates
- Library stamps
- Library bar code stickers / other stickers

Let's go through each of these individually. With the ones I've covered before, I'll direct you to the page where it is covered.

Problem: Library call numbers written on spine

Solution: Old library hardcover books often have their call number actually written on the spine in ink – sometimes white, sometimes black. This ink was then covered with clear lacquer to prevent the ink from chipping off.

Start with taking a lacquer-removing solvent and doing a test to insure it does not destroy the color of the book. The best place to do this test is inside the cover, where the fabric folds over into the inside of the book for a quarter to half an inch. Test the solvent there and make sure it doesn't ruin the coloring.

If the color-test goes well, take cotton rag and remove the coat of lacquer from over the call numbers.

Then take a clean rag or cotton swab, apply a light about of nail polish remover, and remove the call numbers.

The results of this can range from imperceptible, to the area where the numbers were becoming somewhat lighter than the rest of the cover.

Problem: Plastic slipcover over the book containing many stickers, a barcode, etc.

Solution: In many cases you can make a book's library origins invisible merely by removing the slipcover.

Often times, the plastic slipcover will carry with it many blemishes, from call numbers to stickers to the library pocket. By removing the slipcover, you can in one swoop remove most or all of these alterations. This can save you a ton of time.

Problem: Library pocket

Solution: You know what these are. Those little manila pockets on the inside cover.

These pockets were applied with rubber cement until the 1970s, at which point the "peel and stick" variety became dominant. Both can be removed in the same fashion.

Lift and remove all parts of the pocket that are not held down with adhesive. Remove with a knife, razor blade, or scissors.

Take a quilting iron or clothes iron and slowly warm the pocket. As it starts to detach from the inside cover, use a Scotty Peeler or spatula to work the pocket free until it is completely removed.

When it's removed, you are often left with marks left by the glue. This can often be worked away with a Scotty Peeler, knife, or micro-spatula. You may literally be removing a layer of paper here, but the result often looks much better than a glue stain.

Problem: A library book plate on the inside cover or first page

See "Book Plates"

Problem: The library has placed ink stamps on the book

Solution: First, see "*Writing or ink on one or more pages.*" This will give you an overview of your eraser options, and methods of removing ink in the general sense.

Sometimes, its as easy as using a Mars Staedtler plastic eraser. That should be your first start.

I am also going to offer you a trick that is specific to library stamps. This sounds too simple, but the first time I tried it I was amazed.

Take a lifting knife, or other fine-edge (but not "sharp") knife. Apply the tip to the ink stamp, and start literally scraping the ink away. You'd be surprised at how well this works. You'll want to apply only as much pressure as is needed to scrape away the ink.

Supplement your scraping afterwards with a Mars Staedtler plastic eraser. With this two pronged attack, you can often remove literally any evidence the ink stamp was ever there.

Problem: Library bar code stickers or other stickers

Solution: Take a micro-spatula or Scott Peeler and delicately start to work it under the sticker. Go slowly and gently, and in most instances you will be able to coax the bar code sticker from the page.

If you find that some of the paper was removed with the sticker, leaving an unsightly blemish, 320 grip sandpaper will help even out the color.

Problem: Your customer thinks you stole a library book

Example: You were unable to disguise the ex-library status of your book. Then someone orders it from you, is convinced you stole it from a library, and leaves negative feedback accusing you of library theft. If you spend any time on Amazon forums, you will hear stories like this. And it's happened to me once.

Solution: Most retired library books will have a "Discard" stamp, indicating the book has been officially retired. However quite often the library will not do this, and that's where the confusion arises.

I ordered a giant rubber stamp of the word "Discard." I glance over any ex-library book, and if there is no "Discard" stamp already applied, I'll stamp it with mine repeatedly. The goal is to make it impossible for even the most blind customer to miss it. Worth the effort to avoid a theft-accusation.

Section VII

Bonus: Other tricks for increasing the value of books & other media

Books, CDs, & DVDS: Using redundant product pages
DVDs: Purchasing incomplete sets
Books: Common books that are worthless individually, but can be batched into sets and sold profitably
CDs & DVDs: Repairing damaged discs
CDs & DVDs: Batching items with missing artwork and selling on eBay

Books, CDs, & DVDs: Utilizing redundant product pages

This is a cool trick that I first mentioned in **Book Sourcing Secrets**. It's not a "condition hack," but it is a way to greatly increase the value of a book, DVD, CD, or really anything else on Amazon. You do this by taking advantage of redundant product pages.

Let's say you have a copy of Rich Dad Poor Dad. There are hundreds of used copies for sale in the top listing, and of course they're selling for a penny.

But go further down the page, and you'll see two more listings for this book n the first page alone. And used copies on one of the pages are going for $5.40. The rank is worse, but that book is in such high demand that a certain percentage of people are going to check the product page that's further down (who knows why), and buy it. The sale won't come as fast, but if it's a high demand book, it will come.

I counted 7 different product pages for the soft cover edition of Rich Dad Poor Dad, that all appeared to be the same. There are countless books (and CDs and DVDs, etc) that have multiple product pages.

Last Christmas I found 10 copies of the book Outliers by Malcolm Gladwell for $6 each at an overstock store. They were selling for about that amount on the main product page for this book on Amazon, so there was no money to be made. But further down the first page of results, there was a second product page where new copies were selling for $25. I sold all ten during two weeks before Christmas.

I do this all the time. Just pay attention to the Sales Rank on whatever product page you choose, and make sure someone is buying it, at least every now and then.

Big disclaimer: It is absolutely crucial that the product page you use matches the item you are selling exactly. Often there will be subtle differences that don't seem important to you, but will be to the buyer. Check page numbers to make sure they match. With films, make sure whatever bonuses the product page is promising are included on your copy. With CDs, make sure that if your listing promises a CD is "remastered" that the CD you're listing is also remastered. These are small details that are important to people, and trouble will result if you don't give attention to these details.

DVDs: Purchasing incomplete sets

This is used when you find a DVD sets missing one or more volumes.

For example, I'm a big fan of the *Great Courses* sets – high-end CD and DVD programs that you often find in incomplete sets. I'll buy them up anytime I see them, and almost always find the missing portions selling individually on eBay or Amazon for pennies.

I'll also do this regularly with any DVD box sets I find that's missing one or more discs. I check Amazon, then set up an eBay alert and wait for a copy of that individual disc to pop up.

Books: Common books that are worthless individually, but can be batched into sets and sold profitably

There are books series' that are abundantly common anywhere there are used books, and have no value when sold individually. Yet I buy them anyway, because of one trick I learned: I can buy them up, wait until I have a complete set, and then sell the set at a price much higher than the sum of its parts.

There are several series I do this with consistently – books that wouldn't even net you 50 cents sold individually, yet will bring $25+ when sold as sets. Keep your eyes open, and you'll start to see what I mean.

CDs & DVDs: Torn shrink-wrap

There is generally a huge price discrepancy between used and new CDs & DVDs. Quite often you will find sealed CDs & DVDs that have taken ten laps around the planet and look quite worse for the wear. This can take the form of large and small tears. These are important to reign in for two reasons:

- Tears can leave an item teetering on the edge of "not new" condition.
- Tears can get much worse in transit if not contained.

Take a small, small dab of Vaseline and smear every so lightly on the case under the torn wrapping. Then flatten the cellophane on top of the Vaseline. This will keep the wrapping adhered to the case.

This is not an excuse to not mention the tears in the condition description. But it will make those tears far less offensive (and barely perceptible) when the order arrives. And, this has the added benefit of keeping the tears from getting worse on its way to your customer.

Use your best judgment with how much tearing is acceptable before an item is no longer New. A certain small amount of tearing is permissible in the eyes of most buyers, but don't test their limits.

CDs & DVDs: Repairing damaged discs

One of the fastest ways to get negative feedback is to ship a DVD or CD that skips.

If you're concerned about whether a disc skips, but don't want to watch / listen to the whole thing to find out (why would you?), there is a solution. Download a free utility called Nero DiscSpeed. In one minute, it will scan any disc for skips and give you its report.

If you have a DVD or CD that skips, you have to either decide it's not worth your time, or refurbish it.

When I bought the entire inventory from a closed video rental store a couple years ago, I had to learn how to clean discs real fast.

The first thing I did was purchase a JFJ Easy Pro Universal CD/DVD Repair Machine. Mine cost me $120 on Amazon. This does a more than adequate job of repairing individual discs.

A couple things to be aware of: They absolutely kill you on the cleaning fluid. I think I paid $40 per bottle, and if you're doing a lot of discs it will be gone before you know it. Also, this machine is not recommended if you're doing high volume. It takes a minute or so per disc, and requires your full attention. For occasional use, it is more than adequate.

When I decided the volume I was doing exceeded the limits of this machine, I sought professional help. I found someone on an Amazon forum with a high-volume refinishing machine, shipped them about 900 DVDs, plus an additional 600 worthless ones he gave me $1 credit each for, so I ended up paying about $300 in actual cash.

Unless you're doing constant high-volume, I suggest outsourcing your cleaning on an as-needed basis and using a JFJ East Pro for individual discs.

CDs & DVDs: Replacing damaged cases

I don't' want to get too elementary here, but a damaged DVD or CD case is no reason to not sell it. Go on eBay and invest in a batch of generic replacement cases. Keep these around for times when you have cases that need replacing.

CD's & DVDs: Batching items with missing artwork and selling on eBay

In the event of DVDs or CDs that have missing artwork, the first thing to know is that these cannot and should not be sold on Amazon. Even if you mention it in the condition description. Amazon's customers just won't put up with it.

Good news is, you can sell case-less discs on eBay. I wouldn't attempt to sell in individual item with missing artwork on eBay, but in batches you can turn otherwise worthless items into a little bit of money. Just be sure to batch by genre. You're pretty much wasting your time if you're trying to sell a batch of CDs that include both the Fat Boys and Santana. No one is going to buy it.

Condition Hacking: Endnotes

It's my hope that using just one of these tricks just one time will more than pay for the price of this book.

There are (almost) as many types of damage as there are types of books, so draw from the "condition hacking toolkit" and mix-and-match as needed.

And if you figure out how to remove crayon, non-yellow highlighting, or maple syrup, I have a box of damaged books here and I'm desperate.

-Peter Valley

Resources

I spent the first few years as an Amazon seller flailing around, clueless. Today I work hard to bring Amazon sellers the book, courses, tools, and articles I wish I'd had years ago.

Let's be honest: There's a lot of mediocre material out there. Between my blog, my books, and my video courses; I always promise zero filler, and 100% dense, actionable information.

Books by Peter Valley:
- *Amazon Autopilot*
- *Book Sourcing Secrets*
- *Blindspot Profits*
- *Condition Hacking*
- *Feedback Mastery*
- *Online Book Arbitrage*
- *Trade-In Arbitrage*

Video courses by Peter Valley:
- *Amazon Altitude*
- *Book Sourcing Secrets*
- *Pricing Mastery*
- *Condition Hacking*
- *Book Sourcing: 1k In A Day*

Tools by Peter Valley:
- *Zen Arbitrage*
- *Zen Trade*
- *Lyquidator*

All are available at www.FBAmastery.com

CPSIA information can be obtained
at www.ICGtesting.com
Printed in the USA
BVHW052109021120
592172BV00008B/108